I0800647

STUDY GUIDE

The Reformed Pastor

Ian Hamilton

LIGONIER MINISTRIES
Renew your Mind.
LIGONIER.ORG | 800-435-4343

421 Ligonier Court, Sanford, FL 32771
E-mail: info@ligonier.org

Printed in the United States of America.

1

Prototypical Reformed Pastor

INTRODUCTION

All pastors are to model the prototypical pastor, Jesus Christ. In this introductory lesson, Rev. Hamilton highlights the distinguishing characteristics of a servant of God with a view to the servant of God, Jesus Christ.

LESSON OBJECTIVES

1. To answer the question, "What is a reformed pastor?"
2. To present Christ as an example for all truly pastoral ministry
3. To instill a deeper devotion and love for God's people

SCRIPTURE READING

For even the Son of Man came not to be served but to serve, and to give his life as a ransom for many.

—Mark 10:45

LECTURE OUTLINE

A. What is a reformed pastor?

1. The term "reformed pastor" will be used throughout this series in the same way Richard Baxter used it in his book *The Reformed Pastor*.
    a. The use of the word "reformed" does not simply point to an adherence to the doctrines of grace.
    b. The use of the word "reformed" places an emphasis on the character of life the doctrines of grace inevitably produce.
2. The reformed pastor is concerned that people will be shaped and styled into the likeness of Christ.

   a. The reformed pastor must model this transformed lifestyle to the people of God.
   b. God's grace is not passive or inert; it is transformative.
   c. The Holy Spirit establishes God's rule and reign in both the hearts and minds of believers.

B. Servitude is the defining mark of the reformed pastor.
   1. The reformed pastor's life is modeled after Jesus Christ.
      a. The Apostle Peter calls Christ the chief Shepherd (1 Peter 5:4).
      b. All undershepherds are therefore to be conformed to Him.
   2. Isaiah 42 is the template for the servant of God: "*Behold my servant*, whom I uphold . . ." (Isa. 42:1).
      a. God's purpose in calling any man into Christian ministry is to lay the template of His Son's life upon his life.
      b. Christ's life was a life of servitude.
         i. Isaiah 42 is a prophecy fulfilled by our Lord and Savior Jesus Christ (Matt. 12:18).
         ii. The Holy Spirit aims to reproduce in us what He first produced in Christ.
         iii. This is even more the case with the men set apart to be servants of Christ as undershepherds in the church of God.
      c. God's pattern for bringing hope into the world has always been to raise up a servant—Jesus Christ.
         i. God's answer to the futility of idolatry is Jesus Christ as a servant. (Is. 41:24, 29; 42:1)
   3. All pastors are to be modeled after the prototypical pastor.
      a. The reformed pastor will have a lifestyle and mind-set of servitude (Mark 10:45; Luke 22:27).
      b. If there is anything that disqualifies a man from pastoral ministry, it's the absence of a servant's heart.
      c. Service, not status, is to be the primary mark of the reformed pastor.

C. Isaiah 42 highlights five distinct characteristics of the reformed pastor as modeled on Christ.
   1. Reformed pastors recognize that they are upheld men: "Behold my servant, *whom I uphold*" (Isa. 42:1).
      a. Jesus Christ was dependent on the Lord's Spirit, and in His humanity He was upheld by the Father.
      b. Reformed pastors are Spirit-dependent servants (Isa. 42:1).
      c. Reformed pastors understand that they can do nothing without the Spirit and so should give God all the glory (Ps. 115:1).

2. Reformed pastors are not self-promoters: *"He will not cry aloud, or lift up his voice, or make it heard in the street"* (Isa. 42:2).
    a. Jesus Christ did not come to be admired for His gifts and abilities.
    b. Paul did not attempt to flaunt his Apostleship but identified himself as a servant (2 Cor. 4:5).
    c. Reformed pastors are to be men who serve the people of God.
3. Reformed pastors are gentle and kind to the weak and needy: "a bruised reed he will not break, a faintly burning wick he will not quench."
    a. Jesus Christ was accessible to the weakest, the poorest, and the most in need during His earthly ministry.
    b. Paul stresses gentleness as an essential characteristic of the Lord's servant (2 Tim. 2:25).
    c. The only quality of His own life to which Christ ever drew attention was His meek and lowly heart (Matt. 11:29).
4. Reformed pastors are undeviatingly faithful: *"He will not grow faint or be discouraged till he has establish justice in the earth"* (Isa. 42:4).
    a. Jesus Christ was the perfect example of faithfulness.
        i. He was obedient unto death, even the death of the cross (Phil. 2:8).
    b. Reformed pastors understand that faithfulness leads to fruitfulness.
        i. If the faithfulness of every Christian pleases and honors God, how much more so the undershepherds in the flock of Christ?
    c. Faithfulness is becoming more costly as the world becomes increasingly anti-Christian.
        i. Christ's life provides the perfect example of faithfulness amid persecution for all Christians, especially pastors.
5. Reformed pastors are sustained by the knowledge that they are dearly loved: *"Behold my servant, whom I uphold, my chosen, in whom my soul delights"* (Isa. 42:1).
    a. The love of the Father sustained Christ during His earthly life and ministry (Matt. 3:17).
    b. God loves His children to the point that He rejoices over them with singing (Zeph. 3:17).
    c. Reformed pastors, sustained by God's love, should take the greatest joy to be in service to all those dearly loved by God.
        i. One of the principal notes of the reformed pastor will be to help his people understand God's love for them.

STUDY QUESTIONS

1. Richard Baxter titled his work *The Reformed Pastor* to stress the gospel minister's understanding of the doctrines of grace.
    a. True
    b. False

2. The only personal characteristics to which Jesus draws attention in the gospel of Matthew are ________ and lowliness of heart.
   a. Kindness
   b. Loveliness
   c. Meekness
   d. Gentleness

3. Isaiah 42 is commonly understood as one of Isaiah's ________ Songs.
   a. Suffering
   b. Prophetic
   c. Messianic
   d. Servant

4. Status is a primary mark of the reformed pastor.
   a. True
   b. False

5. Reformed pastors understand that ________ is the source of ministerial fruitfulness.
   a. Prayer
   b. Fasting
   c. Faithfulness
   d. All of the above

6. Jesus Christ is *the* ________.
   a. Pastor
   b. Shepherd
   c. Servant of God
   d. All of the above

DISCUSSION QUESTIONS

1. What are the primary characteristics of the Servant of God in Isaiah 42?

2. Christ did not come to make a name for Himself. How should this influence your view of Christian ministry?

3. Where did Christ's faithfulness lead Him? What are the implications of this on the Christian life?

4. Why is the reformed pastor obliged to give all glory to God?

2

The Reformed Pastor's Spirituality

INTRODUCTION

Samuel Rutherford's greatest legacy to the Christian church is his pastoral letters. In this lesson, Rev. Hamilton focuses on the themes of these letters to show how they reveal the common features of a reformed pastor's spiritual life.

LESSON OBJECTIVES

1. To underline the themes found throughout Samuel Rutherford's pastoral letters
2. To connect these themes to the life and ministry of every reformed pastor

SCRIPTURE READING

. . . so that we may be able to comfort those who are in any affliction, with the comfort with which we ourselves are comforted by God.

—2 Cor. 1:4b

LECTURE OUTLINE

A. Samuel Rutherford's greatest legacy to the Christian church is his pastoral letters.
   1. Samuel Rutherford (1600–1661) was a Scottish pastor-theologian.
      a. He was committed to the doctrines of grace and was involved in the formation of the Westminster Standards.
   2. Rutherford's warm letters prove that cold Calvinism is a theological oxymoron.
   3. Throughout Rutherford's many letters, a number of themes surface that reveal the hallmarks of reformed piety.

B. Reformed pastors are supremely Christocentric.
   1. Jesus Christ is the thematic centerpiece of almost all of Rutherford's letters.

    a. Rutherford's letters in 1637 provide many examples of his Christ-centeredness.
2. Rutherford was a theologian of the highest caliber, but he understood that the gospel was to be accessible, and the heart of the gospel is Jesus Christ.
3. It deeply grieved Rutherford that so few saw how lovely Jesus Christ was in His person and work.

C. Reformed pastors have a deep concern for the souls of their people.
1. Rutherford had a passionate care for the eternal well being of his people.
    a. The reality of eternity is a marked characteristic of Puritan piety.
2. Rutherford believed that he needed to confront people with eternity.
3. Rutherford's letters greatly inspired the hymn writer Anne Ross Cousin.
4. The concern for the souls of men is not merely a common feature of the reformed pastor but of the Lord Jesus Christ.
    a. Christ wept for Jerusalem (Matt. 23; Luke 13; Luke 19)
    b. Paul's heart is that Israel would be saved and that even he would be accursed if it meant their salvation (Rom. 9–10).
5. Rutherford understood that the doctrines of predestination and election did not do away with the reformed pastor's overwhelming concern for the souls of men and women.

D. Reformed pastors have a deep sense of the sinfulness of sin.
1. Rutherford was most deeply conscious of his own sin.
    a. The Apostle Paul called himself "the chief of sinners" (1 Tim. 1:15) and "less than the least of all the saints" (Eph. 3:8).
2. It deeply troubled Rutherford that he could be admired as a master of the spiritual life.
    a. Only those with a deep sense of their own sinfulness before God can be effective ministers of the truth of God's grace to others.
3. Rutherford wanted to turn people's attention away from himself and to Christ.
    a. Rutherford was an incredibly able theologian, but he was not pulled into the temptations common to today's evangelical celebrity culture.

E. Reformed pastors are full of counsel to afflicted saints.
1. Tender compassion and strong counsel are distinguishing features throughout Rutherford's 350 extant letters.
2. Rutherford understood the nature of the tenderhearted Savior as described in Isaiah 42.
3. Rutherford's counsel may have been so profound because he wrote out of deep personal suffering and anguish.
    a. Rutherford was not writing abstractly or clinically.
        i. He had difficult family circumstances.
        ii. He was also exiled to the far north of Scotland for preaching the gospel.

   b. Rutherford's circumstances gave him close fellowship with afflicted Christians.

F. Reformed pastors are full of eagerness for heaven.
   1. The center of Rutherford's life lay in heaven, not on earth.
   2. Rutherford's language drew heavily on the Song of Songs in his longing expectation of the marriage day.
      a. He understood the Song of Songs as portraying the Savior's relationship with His church.
      b. This relationship finds its fullest flower in the New Testament where Christ gave himself up for her.
      c. Jesus Christ is everything in the life of the reformed pastor because of what He has done for His church.

STUDY QUESTIONS

1. Samuel Rutherford ministered in the sixteenth century.
   a. True
   b. False

2. ________ Calvinism is a theological oxymoron.
   a. New
   b. Cold
   c. Hyper
   d. Caged

3. Rutherford believed that he had to confront people with ________.
   a. Sin
   b. Christ
   c. Sovereignty
   d. Eternity

4. Rutherford's profound spiritual counsel can be attributed to his ________.
   a. Study
   b. Suffering
   c. Love
   d. Devotion

5. Rutherford enjoyed a peaceful and quiet life because he faithfully preached the gospel.
   a. True
   b. False

6. Rutherford played a role in the development of the ________.
   a. Belgic Confession
   b. Canons of Dort
   c. Heidelberg Catechism
   d. Westminster Standards

DISCUSSION QUESTIONS

1. How does Rutherford's letters betray the lie that Calvinism is cold, hard, and clinical?

2. What key features of the reformed pastor strike out against the notion that Calvinists are not evangelists? Where can we find support for this throughout the lives of Jesus Christ and the apostle Paul?

3. Samuel Rutherford, like the apostle Paul, had a keen understanding of his own vileness. In what ways does knowledge of personal sin help the reformed pastor?

4. What suffering has God providentially brought into your life that may be used to minister to others?

3

The Fellowship of the Saints

INTRODUCTION

The ordinary means of grace do not take place in a vacuum. In this lesson, Rev. Hamilton relays the importance of the fellowship of the saints as the very context in which the ordinary means of grace operate to the salvation of God's people.

LESSON OBJECTIVE

1. To stress the importance of the local congregation as the place where the ordinary means of grace are at work

SCRIPTURE READING

. . . not neglecting to meet together, as is the habit of some . . .

—Hebrews 10:25a

LECTURE OUTLINE

A. Reformed pastors must build God's church according to God's revealed will.
   1. Reformed pastors are called to "preach the word in season and out of season" (2 Tim. 2:4).
      a. Though we live in turbulent and changing times, reformed pastors are not swayed by the winds of culture.
   2. The gospel of God's grace through Jesus Christ is transgenerational.
      a. This is rooted in the fact that God is transgenerational.
      b. God has instructed us in the ways to build His church.
      c. God is the chief church builder.

B. Reformed churches have always believed that God saves and sanctifies His people through the ordinary means of grace.
   1. The ordinary means of grace are the Word faithfully preached, the sacraments rightly administered, and the exercise of prayer, praise, and church discipline.
   2. The ordinary means of grace have both an ultimate and a proximate purpose.
      a. God's ultimate purpose concerns the glory of His Son.
         i. This does involve our conformity to Christ, but ultimately, it is so that Christ would be "the firstborn among many brothers" (Rom. 8:29).
      b. God's proximate purpose is to conform us to Christ.
         i. He does this supremely by the ordinary means of grace.

C. The principal context of the ordinary means of grace is the fellowship of the saints.
   1. Today, many Christians no longer think instinctively in corporate and covenantal terms.
      a. We need to be reminded of the centrality and importance of the church.
   2. Christ's response to the disciples' request that He teach them to pray is a helpful reminder of the emphasis that needs to be placed on fellowship.
      a. He did not teach them to pray, "*My* Father," but "*Our* Father."
      b. When someone is saved by the grace of God, they are brought into the fellowship of the people of God.
   3. Paul writes that comprehending the love of God takes place in the context "with all the saints" (Eph. 3:19).
   4. The church is the supreme and only context in which the means of grace operate to our sanctification.

D. Christ endowed the church with all kinds of spiritual gifts for the edification and the building up into one body.
   1. Christ gave the church "the apostles, the prophets, the evangelists, the shepherds, and teachers" (Eph. 4:11).
      a. This is to "equip the saints for the work of ministry" (Eph. 4:12—14).
      b. Beyond this, these gifts are so "that we may no longer be children tossed to and fro" (Eph. 4:14–16).
         i. Christians who are connected to the body of Christ will not be overwhelmed.
         ii. In order to grow in Christ, Christians need to be where the ordinary means of grace are ministered.
   2. The significance of the church in the sanctification of God's people was a dominant theme in the writings of the Magisterial Reformers.
      a. John Calvin wrote, "so that for those of whom God is Father, the church may also be mother."
         i. Calvin is simply echoing the teaching of God's Word.

E. The corporate and covenantal aspect of Christ's church has existed from its beginning.
   1. A striking feature of the old covenant is that its people did not live as isolated individuals.
   2. A striking feature of the new covenant, from its inception, is that it continues in the same corporate dimensions of the old.
      a. Those that were joined to the church immediately devoted themselves to fellowship (Acts 2:42).
      b. The English word *fellowship*—or *communion*—comes from the Greek word *koinōnia*.
         i. *Koinōnia* is used to describe the marriage relationship.
         ii. Christians are bonded together as the people of God united to Christ.
   3. The example of the early Christians who immediately attached to and continued in fellowship guards against the individualism of today.
      a. They honored the only institution established by our Lord Jesus Christ.
      b. The lives of believers who do not join themselves to a local church display the necessity of doing so.
      c. Christians need the encouragement, support, comfort, and ministry that come from the fellowship of God's people.
   4. The Enlightenment exalted the individual, but the teaching of Scripture is that we are one people of God.
      a. Individualism harms the gospel and cause of Christ (John 13:35).
      b. There is safety and power in community (Matt. 16:18).
      c. Christians should commit themselves to a local church that is faithful to the ordinary means of grace and not by a standard based on personal preferences.
   5. Reformation Christianity labored to set justifying grace and imputed righteousness in their biblical, covenantal, and corporate context.
      a. Justifying grace naturally brings you into fellowship with the body of Christ, His church.
      b. Christians are unified in Christ and are thus called to love one another (John 13:35).

STUDY QUESTIONS

1. The significance of the church with respect to the sanctification of God's people was a minor point during the Reformation.
   a. True
   b. False

2. The ________ is an institution established by the Lord Jesus Christ.
   a. Church
   b. Lord's Supper
   c. Sacrament of baptism
   d. All of the above

3. The ________ exalted the individual.
   a. French Revolution
   b. American Revolution
   c. Reformation
   d. Enlightenment

4. Many Christians no longer think in covenantal and ________ terms.
   a. Systematic
   b. Corporate
   c. Calvinistic
   d. Individualistic

5. The ________ is the only context in which the means of grace operate to our sanctification.
   a. Heart
   b. Head
   c. Church
   d. All of the above

6. The idea that the church is our mother is exclusively Roman Catholic.
   a. True
   b. False

DISCUSSION QUESTIONS

1. The gospel of God in Jesus Christ is transgenerational. What are the implications of this truth on how we are to build His church according to His Word?

2. How can you correct someone who believes he is surviving well enough on his own as a Christian outside of the church? What dangers does Scripture warn against when it comes to the isolated Christian?

3. What great Christian apologetic do we miss out on if we fall into the individualistic trappings of our day?

4. What is the significance of the use of the Greek term *koinōnia* to describe the union between a husband and a wife?

4

The Ordinary Means of Grace

INTRODUCTION

God works through the ordinary means of grace by blessing them with His Spirit. In this lecture, Rev. Hamilton explores the ministry of the Holy Spirit in the life of Jesus Christ, its parallel work in the lives of believers, and the reformed pastor's heartfelt dependence on it.

LESSON OBJECTIVES

1. To emphasize the essential cooperation of both Word and Spirit through the ordinary means of grace
2. To show how the work of the Spirit in the life of Christ is the same as His work in the life of the believer
3. To facilitate an understanding that the reformed pastor can do nothing without the Holy Spirit

SCRIPTURE READING

By the Holy Spirit who dwells within us, guard the good deposit entrusted to you.

—2 Timothy 1:14

LECTURE OUTLINE

A. God's usual means of beautifying His children is through the ministry of His Word.

1. The Word is preached, made visible in the sacraments, and voiced in prayer and singing to God.
2. It is through the ordinary means of grace that the Holy Spirit makes us more like Christ.

    a. What the Spirit first produced in Christ, he reproduces in the people of Christ.
    b. John Calvin referred to this as the Holy Spirit's "ministry of replication."
  3. To appreciate the Spirit's sanctifying work in the believer, the Spirit's sanctifying work in Christ through the Word must be first understood.

B. The Word of God was absolutely instrumental in the developmental sanctification of our Lord Jesus Christ.
  1. Christ's sanctification was both definitive and progressive.
    a. Jesus was set apart in His mother's womb (Luke 1:35; Heb. 7:26).
    b. Jesus also increased in wisdom and learned obedience (Luke 2:52; Heb. 5:8).
  2. Jesus increased in wisdom by living under the Word of God.
    a. Jesus is described as "one who is taught" (Isa. 50:4).
    b. Jesus needed the Father to open His ears (Isa. 50:4).
  3. Jesus was dependent on the Word of God.
    a. Jesus fought the temptations of the devil with the Word of God (Matt. 4:1–11; Duet. 8:3, 6:13, 6:16).
    b. Jesus learned from the Word of God.
      i. His humanity is our humanity.

C. The Spirit reproduces in the Christian what He first produced in Christ.
  1. Jesus prayed to the Father that we would be sanctified by the truth (John 17:17).
    a. It is not merely that we would know the truth but be sanctified by it through the working of the Holy Spirit.
  2. The Word of God keeps us from sinning (Ps. 119:11).
    a. The Word must be applied by the mortifying, vivifying work of the Holy Spirit.
  3. The Lord needs to open our eyes that we would follow His instruction (Ps. 119:18).
  4. The Word cannot be separated from the Spirit.
    a. The Spirit alone comprehends the thoughts of God (1 Cor. 2:9–12).
    b. We would remain in darkness without the ministry of the Holy Spirit.
  5. Dependence on the Holy Spirit is the subtext of the ordinary means of grace.
    a. Word and Spirit belong inextricably together.

D. The reformed pastor understands the importance of the internal ministry of the Holy Spirit.
  1. B.B. Warfield considered Calvin's doctrine of the Holy Spirit to be his greatest contribution to the work of the Reformation.
  2. It is not enough to preach the Word accurately.
    a. The great means of grace is the Word of God as it is blessed and quickened by the Spirit of God.
    b. The Lord must grant the grace of the new birth in order for someone to truly hear Christ.

    c. The account of Philip and the Ethiopian eunuch is a great example of the eye-opening work of God's Spirit (Acts 8:26–40).
3. Reformed pastors understand that they can accomplish nothing without the ministry of the Holy Spirit.
    a. They believe that the Holy Spirit will take the Word of truth and apply it to the lives of the people of God unto their salvation.
    b. If the Word and Spirit are separated, the Word is severed from its life-giving power.
    c. The Holy Spirit seeks to conform us to the written revelation of God so that we may know Him and the beauty of our Savior Jesus Christ.
4. When Paul exhorts Timothy to "preach the word," Timothy understands that Paul means in utter dependence on the Holy Spirit (1 Tim. 4:2).
    a. The Word of God is the sword of the Spirit (Eph. 6:17).
    b. The Word of God makes us wise unto salvation (2 Tim. 3:15).
    c. The Word of God is a lamp to our feet and a light to our path (Ps. 119:105).
5. The great work of a reformed pastor is to preach the Word in absolute heartfelt dependence on the Holy Spirit.

STUDY QUESTIONS

1. John Calvin refers to the Holy Spirit's ministry of ________ as the work in which the Spirit works in us what He first worked in Christ.
    a. Repetition
    b. Reproduction
    c. Duplication
    d. Replication

2. The Word of God, without the Holy Spirit, is sufficient for the salvation and sanctification of God's people.
    a. True
    b. False

3. B.B. Warfield believed ________ doctrine of the Holy Spirit was his greatest contribution to the Reformation.
    a. John Owen's
    b. John Calvin's
    c. Martin Luther's
    d. Abraham Kuyper's

4. Christ's sanctification was only definitive.
    a. True
    b. False

5. Just as those who follow Him, Christ was sustained by the ________.
    a. Father
    b. Holy Spirit
    c. Word of God
    d. All of the above

6. The Reformed pastor understands the ________ ministry and witness of the Holy Spirit.
    a. Essential
    b. Powerful
    c. Internal
    d. Present

DISCUSSION QUESTIONS

1. Since the Word of God is the central element of the ordinary means of grace, what should the reformed pastor expect in studying and teaching it to others?

2. How should the Christian resist the devil's temptations?

3. What essential truth does Christ's dependence on the Word of God for His sanctification teach us about Him?

4. How effective would the reformed pastor be without the work of the Holy Spirit? Why?

5

The Reformed Congregation

INTRODUCTION

The reformed pastor is called to shepherd the flock as one who must give an account. In this lesson, Rev. Hamilton describes the reformed pastor's love for his congregation as expressed through the intimacy of pastoral visitation.

LESSON OBJECTIVES

1. To place priority on the congregation as a focal point for truly pastoral ministry
2. To answer the why, when, and how of pastoral visitation

SCRIPTURE READING

The good shepherd lays his life down for the sheep.

—John 10:11b

LECTURE OUTLINE

A. Reformed pastors are called to know their flocks.
   1. The Reformation recovered more than the doctrines of grace; it also recovered the pastor's care for his flock.
   2. Reformed pastors should be able to say, along with Christ, "I know my sheep" (John 10:14).
   3. Pastors can get to know the people they are called to serve by visiting them.

B. Why should reformed pastors visit their flocks?
   1. God commands it.
      a. The apostle Paul taught from house to house (Acts 20:20).
         i. Calvin believed this verse proved that house-to-house visitation was a mark of a true pastor.

   b. Pastors need to be creative in how they navigate cultural changes while maintaining their intimacy with those they are called to serve.
2. Pastors will gain an understanding of their flocks.
   a. Pastors will become familiar with the idiosyncrasies, needs, longings, fears, hopes, and joys of their flocks.
   b. Pastors will see their congregations as consisting of unique individuals.
3. Pastors will know how to apply the Word of God to their flocks.
   a. Application is applying the balm of Christ where it hurts and the rebukes of Christ where needed.
      i. It is done principally through the preaching of the Word.
      ii. Pastors will understand whether the congregation has rightly grasped what has been preached by visiting with them.
4. Pastors will expose their humanity to their flocks
   a. Pastors are sheep before they are shepherds.
      i. It is not a stranger who is preaching to them every Sunday, but a brother who is coming alongside them.
      ii. Jesus Christ has made us all brothers (Heb. 2:11–13).
5. Pastors will cultivate the peace and harmony of their flocks.
   a. Consistent visitation has the capacity to defuse potential time bombs.
   b. Consistent visitation will help in anticipating and addressing the concerns of the congregation.
6. Pastors will find the fruit of the Word among their flocks.
   a. Richard Baxter personally experienced the impact that close discourse could have among his people.
   b. Pastors can never take for granted that their flocks are actually receiving what is being preached.
   c. Sometimes it is only when a pastor visits face-to-face that people will begin to honestly disclose what's inside then.
7. Pastors must be wise and creative in order to pursue their calling as perfectly exemplified by Christ.
   a. In some situations it may not be appropriate to visit in homes.
      i. Pastors must be creative in order to minister to single women by visiting them in public places or in appropriate company.

C. How should reformed pastors visit their flocks?
1. Pastors should visit their flocks as shepherds who are sheep.
   a. Pastors are not to lord over their flocks but to serve them in accordance with Christ (Mark 10:45; Luke 22:27; 1 Peter 5:3).
   b. Pastors are forgiven sinners.
      i. They are not above the flock in this sense.
   c. Pastors have been given the weighty commission to preach the Word of God and to exercise godly oversight over the flock.

            i. When a congregation recognizes this, it profoundly influences how they hear the preached Word.
    2. Pastors should visit willingly.
        a. Pastors are to be willing servants of God's people.
        b. The Christian life may not be easy, but it is simple.
            i. We are called to love God.
        c. The Christian life may be simple, but it is not easy.
            i. We are called to put sin to death.
            ii. Jesus Christ gave His life for the flock.
            iii. Pastors must learn to give up their time to minister the grace of God to their flocks.
    3. Pastors should visit as servants.
        a. If the chief Shepherd was a servant to the flock, the reformed pastor cannot be otherwise.
    4. Pastors should visit wisely.
        a. Some visits cannot be done alone and require the company of an elder or other members of the congregation.
        b. One of the qualifications of an elder is being hospitable (1 Tim. 3:2).
            i. The home should be a hospital, especially used if visitations are difficult.
    5. Pastors should seek to visit members in a familial context.
        a. When pastors visit families they can sense the family dynamics that may not be apparent on Sundays.
    6. Pastors should visit gently.
        a. The Lord Jesus does not break bruised reeds (Isa. 42:3).
        b. An overbearing man would be disqualified from the pastorate.
        c. Reformed pastors seek to have their lives shaped by the gentleness of the Savior.

D. When should reformed pastors visit?
    1. Pastors should visit regularly.
        a. Deep needs are not always obvious and might only surface through regular visits.
        b. There is no precise pattern to every time and place.
            i. The pastor must be creative in fulfilling his call in the context in which he is placed.
    2. Pastors should visit idiosyncratically.
        a. Pastors must understand the people they are visiting and the ideal frequency between visits.
            i. Some people live untroubled lives, and some people need more regular visits.
        b. Pastoral visits do not necessarily need to be long or involved.
        c. Pastoral visits do not require a reason.

  i. The people are the flock of God and the pastor will one day have to give an account (Heb. 13:17).
  ii. Pastoral visits may prevent the familial breakdowns—that on the surface appear doctrinal—within a congregation.

E. Pastoral visitation should be a great priority for any pastor called by God to reflect the oversight and care of Jesus Christ.

1. Christ knew His sheep in a way no pastor ever could, but He gave Himself on earth to knowing His flock, as the reformed pastor should do too.

STUDY QUESTIONS

1. ________ is essential to pastoral visitation.
   a. Intimacy
   b. Regularity
   c. Creativity
   d. All of the above

2. There is a specific text of Scripture that commands that pastors must visit the members of their church.
   a. True
   b. False

3. ________ believed that there were seven types of people within every congregation
   a. Samuel Rutherford
   b. John Owen
   c. William Perkins
   d. Richard Baxter

4. The relationship of the pastor to his people is based on the fact that Jesus Christ has ________ us in the gospel.
   a. Saved
   b. Betrothed
   c. Brothered
   d. All of the above

5. The key qualification of an elder that should be kept in mind in creating ways to be with God's people is ________.
   a. Sober-mindedness
   b. Hospitality
   c. Gentleness
   d. Self-control

6. Oftentimes the divisions within a church appear to be familial but are actually doctrinal.
   a. True
   b. False

DISCUSSION QUESTIONS

1. Why does Rev. Hamilton place a high priority on pastoral visitation?

2. How do we conclude from Scripture that pastors are to visit their people?

3. What sort of situations might require the reformed pastor to employ creativity in visiting with his people?

4. How may a congregation come to realize the weight placed on the reformed pastor to preach the Word of God and to exercise oversight?

6

John Calvin: Reformed Pastor

INTRODUCTION

John Calvin sought before God to be a faithful pastor and is thus a model for the reformed pastor. In this final lesson, Rev. Hamilton points us to Christ as the heart of Calvin's theology, ministry, and life.

LESSON OBJECTIVES

1. To communicate the defining marks of John Calvin's pastoral ministry

SCRIPTURE READING

. . . whoever serves, as one who serves by the strength that God supplies . . .

—1 Peter 4:11b

LECTURE OUTLINE

A. John Calvin is a model pastor for the reformed pastor to emulate.
   1. Calvin's motto: "My heart I give to you, oh Lord, promptly and sincerely."
      a. Calvin sought before God to be a faithful pastor.
   2. Calvin believed it was his duty to "take charge of every particular sheep."
      a. Richard Baxter derived his conviction of house-to-house visitations from John Calvin.
      b. Calvin derived it from the apostle Paul (Acts 20:20).
   3. Calvin was deeply concerned to know all of his flock by name and need.
      a. This echoes the words of our Savior (John 10:3).

B. John Calvin was convinced that love for Christ is at the heart of truly pastoral ministry.
   1. Calvin believed that love for Christ was the only way a pastor could be faithful to his office.
      a. Christ's words to Peter: "Do you love me? Feed my sheep" (John 21:15).
      b. Love for Christ is the one indispensible quality needed to be a pastor.
         i. If love for Christ is absent, then everything is absent.
   2. Love for Christ is the foundation for a pastor's usefulness.
      a. Jesus asked Simon three times, "Do you love me?" (John 21:15).
      b. Perhaps this is a question that search committees should be asking potential pastors: "Do you love Christ?"

C. John Calvin's pastoral ministry reflected the servant's spirit of Jesus Christ.
   1. All pastors are nothing more than servants of believers (2 Cor. 4:5).
      a. Serving the people of God is the highest honor to which a pastor can aspire.
   2. Calvin lived out this conviction as a minister to the people of Geneva.
      a. Calvin was dismissed from Geneva in 1538.
      b. He was asked to return by the people two and a half years later.
      c. Calvin was initially reluctant to the possibility of returning to Geneva, but when he received the actual request for his return, he assumed his role as a servant of God's people.
      d. Calvin began preaching right where he left off.

D. John Calvin never wearied of telling his congregation to look to Christ.
   1. Calvin believed that the only hope for his people was that they look away from themselves to Christ.
      a. Samuel Rutherford echoed this sentiment: "For every one look you take to yourself, take ten looks at Christ."
      b. Our standing before God is eternally secure in Christ, yet one of Satan's great designs is to turn our gaze into ourselves.
         i. Luther even defined sin as "that which turns you in upon yourself."
         ii. The devil schemes to turn the Christian in upon himself through flattery and accusation.
   2. A fixed gaze on Christ was a consistent theme of Calvin's pastoral counsel.
      a. To be a gospel missionary in France during the 1540s and 1550s was a death sentence.
      b. Calvin wrote to the young men waiting on death row in Chambéry that Christ would supply them with every virtue.
      c. Calvin also emphasized the fatherliness of God.
         i. The Lord Jesus Christ commanded His disciples to call upon their Father.

- ii. There are more references to God as "Father" in the sixth chapter of Matthew than in the entire Old Testament.
- iii. The revelation of God's glorious Fatherhood comes in the new covenant through Christ.

3. Calvin's concern was that believers would be comforted and, ultimately, that God might be honored and glorified.
   - a. All of our comforts dwell in the Lord, and He supplies us with all things (1 Cor. 4:7; Ps. 115:1).
4. The weightiest obligation of the reformed pastor is to point people to Christ.
   - a. If we believe that salvation is all of grace and no good thing dwells in us, then we make no contribution to our salvation except the sin that necessitates our salvation.

E. John Calvin's pastoral ministry reflected the overflow of union with Christ.

1. Calvin understood that the Lord Jesus Christ is the church's true and chief Pastor.
   - a. Christ's life was marked by death and resurrection, and these should be the true marks of the reformed pastor (John 12:23–26).
2. Union with Christ consists of union with both His humiliation and exaltation—the suffering and the glory.
   - a. Calvin's emphasis was that "the cross came before the crown," and so it is in Christian ministry.
   - b. The grace of the gospel introduces us to union with Christ and thus the sufferings of Christ.
3. Calvin understood that the willingness to die was the foundational principle of spiritual fruitfulness.
   - a. Paul highlighted that pastoral ministry is a matter of death that brings to life (2 Cor. 4:7–12).
   - b. This life uniquely came out of the sufferings of Christ (1 Peter 3:18).
   - c. Christ's pattern is the pattern for all Christians and pastors, and this is the pattern Calvin followed in returning to Geneva in 1541.
     - i. Calvin was taking up his cross, a requirement of all of Christ's disciples (Luke 9:23).
   - d. The Christian's readiness to die is a stark reality for our Christian brothers and sisters in Iran and Syria.
4. Union with Christ means that the reformed pastor must die to himself.
   - a. The death of a ministry is when a pastor begins to believe he is actually something more than a servant of God's people.
   - b. The reformed pastor must die to pride, financial gain, recognition, and approval in step with the principle that death brings forth life.
   - c. In the words of Christ, "I am among you as one who serves" (Luke 22:27).

STUDY QUESTIONS

1. "My heart I give to you, oh Lord, promptly and sincerely" was the motto of ________.
   a. Samuel Rutherford
   b. Richard Baxter
   c. John Calvin
   d. John Owen

2. Calvin derived from Richard Baxter his conviction that pastors should visit from house to house in order to address the needs of God's people.
   a. True
   b. False

3. Pastors are the ________ of believers.
   a. Shepherds
   b. Teachers
   c. Servants
   d. All of the above

4. ________ defined sin as "that which turns you in upon yourself."
   a. John Owen
   b. John Calvin
   c. Samuel Rutherford
   d. Martin Luther

5. Calvin encouraged men on death row in Chambéry to look to God as ________.
   a. Sovereign
   b. Father
   c. Savior
   d. King

6. According to Calvin, union with Christ implies dying to self..
   a. True
   b. False

DISCUSSION QUESTIONS

1. What do Christ's words to Peter, "Do you love me? Feed my sheep," teach the reformed pastor?

2. In what ways does the devil attempt to distract the believer's eyes away from Christ?

3. What does union with Christ primarily teach the reformed pastor about how he is to pattern his life and ministry?

4. Calvin said of Geneva, “There is no place under heaven in which I have a greater dread.” What does his willingness to return to Geneva tell us about his understanding of pastoral ministry?

Answer Key for Study Questions

Lesson 1
1. b
2. c
3. d
4. b
5. c
6. d

Lesson 2
1. b
2. b
3. d
4. b
5. b
6. d

Lesson 3
1. b
2. a
3. d
4. b
5. c
6. a

Lesson 4
1. d
2. b
3. b
4. b
5. d
6. c

Lesson 5
1. d
2. b
3. c
4. c
5. b
6. b

Lesson 6
1. c
2. b
3. d
4. d
5. b
6. a